A Guide to
AMERICAN STATES

# Oklahoma

## THE SOONER STATE

www.av2books.com

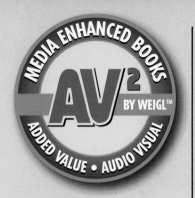

AV² provides enriched content that supplements and complements this book. Weigl's AV² books strive to create inspired learning and engage young minds in a total learning experience.

## Your AV² Media Enhanced books come alive with...

**Audio**
Listen to sections of the book read aloud.

**Key Words**
Study vocabulary, and complete a matching word activity.

**Video**
Watch informative video clips.

**Quizzes**
Test your knowledge.

**Embedded Weblinks**
Gain additional information for research.

**Slide Show**
View images and captions, and prepare a presentation.

**Try This!**
Complete activities and hands-on experiments.

**... and much, much more!**

Go to **www.av2books.com**, and enter this book's unique code.

**BOOK CODE**

C 4 9 0 8 1 5

**AV² by Weigl** brings you media enhanced books that support active learning.

Published by AV² by Weigl
350 5th Avenue, 59th Floor
New York, NY 10118
Website: www.av2books.com     www.weigl.com

Library of Congress Cataloging-in-Publication Data

Strudwick, Leslie, 1970-
 Oklahoma / Leslie Strudwick.
     p. cm. -- (A guide to American states)
 Includes index.
 ISBN 978-1-61690-808-9 (hardcover : alk. paper) -- ISBN 978-1-61690-484-5 (online)
 1. Oklahoma--Juvenile literature. I. Title.
 F694.3.S775 2011
 976.6--dc23
                          2011019025

Printed in the United States of America in North Mankato, Minnesota

052011
WEP180511

Project Coordinator  Jordan McGill
Art Director  Terry Paulhus

Photo Credits
Every reasonable effort has been made to trace ownership and to obtain permission to reprint copyright material. The publishers would be pleased to have any errors or omissions brought to their attention so that they may be corrected in subsequent printings.

Weigl acknowledges Getty Images as its primary image supplier for this title.

# Contents

*Around 1.1 million people call Oklahoma City and its surrounding area home. The city is a fascinating blend of hip, urban culture and deep western heritage.*

# Introduction

O klahoma occupies a unique place in U.S. history. In the mid-1800s, as the United States pushed westward, the land that would later become Oklahoma remained mostly untouched by settlers. The U.S. government had set the area aside as Indian Territory. It was a home for various American Indian peoples forced off their homelands. The state's American Indian **heritage** shows even in its name. "Oklahoma" is a combination of two Choctaw Indian words, *okla*, meaning "people," and *humma*, meaning "red."

Although Oklahoma is usually thought to consist of flat prairies, the state is truly breathtaking. Its terrain is **diverse**, with mountains as well as vast level plains.

Northwestern Oklahoma is a long narrow strip of land called the Panhandle. Isolated hills called buttes and flat-topped hills called mesas cover the Panhandle's dry western landscape.

Oklahoma has more than 55,000 miles of shoreline along lakes and ponds. Eucha Lake, in northeastern Oklahoma, has 45 miles of shoreline.

In addition to American Indians, Oklahoma's land has been inhabited by pioneers, cowboys, and outlaws. All have contributed to the state's rich past, paving the way to the present.

Oklahoma was one of the last states to join the Union. It was admitted on November 16, 1907, becoming the 46th state. Since then, Oklahoma has achieved an integration of its American Indian citizens into modern life that probably is unmatched by any other state. Oklahomans who have achieved positions of distinction in their chosen fields include many people of American Indian heritage.

Once largely agricultural, the economy of Oklahoma today is a blend of agriculture and other industries. Cowboys, rodeos, and country-music singers highlight Oklahoma's ranching history, while oil wells reflect the importance of the energy industry to the modern state.

# Where Is Oklahoma?

**O**klahoma lies in the south-central portion of the United States. Three interstate highways pass through Oklahoma City, dividing the state north-south, east-west, and northeast-southwest. Oklahoma City and Tulsa have international airports. Numerous regional, municipal, and private airports are scattered throughout the state.

*Will Rogers World Airport serves the Oklahoma City area. More than 3 million passengers a year use the airport. Six major airlines provide transportation on the airport's three runways.*

Oklahoma has an unusual nickname, the Sooner State. This nickname refers to the land-hungry settlers who came to the area during the Great Land Rush in 1889. Although much of Oklahoma's land was reserved for American Indians, the government made a section of land available to new settlers. Newcomers were told to line up at the Oklahoma border and, at the signal, race to claim the land. Those who jumped the starting gun were called Sooners.

Boomer's Paradise is another early nickname for Oklahoma. This name refers to the people who illegally entered American Indian territory. They set up homes and communities on these reserved lands. These nicknames serve as reminders of Oklahoma's early history, when American Indians and settlers were wrestling over land and resources.

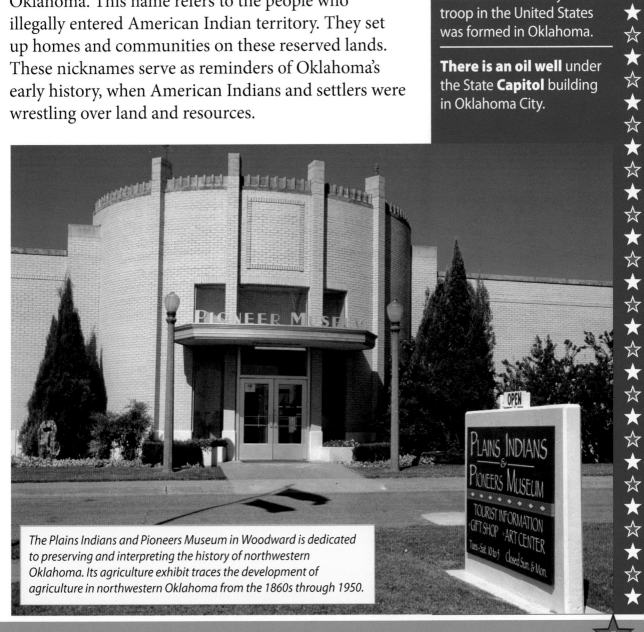

The Plains Indians and Pioneers Museum in Woodward is dedicated to preserving and interpreting the history of northwestern Oklahoma. Its agriculture exhibit traces the development of agriculture in northwestern Oklahoma from the 1860s through 1950.

# Mapping Oklahoma

**O**klahoma shares borders with six other states. Arkansas and Missouri lie to the east, and Kansas and Colorado are to the north. New Mexico is to the west, and Texas is to the south. The Red River forms most of Oklahoma's southern border with Texas. Other important rivers are the Arkansas, the Canadian, and the Washita.

## Sites and Symbols

**STATE SEAL**
Oklahoma

**STATE BIRD**
Scissor-tailed Flycatcher

**STATE WILDFLOWER**
Indian Blanket

**STATE FLAG**
Oklahoma

**STATE ANIMAL**
American Buffalo

**STATE TREE**
Redbud

**Nickname** The Sooner State

**Motto** *Labor Omnia Vincit* (Labor Conquers All Things)

**Song** "Oklahoma!" words by Oscar Hammerstein and music by Richard Rodgers

**Entered the Union** November 16, 1907, as the 46th state

**Capital** Oklahoma City

**Population** (2010 Census) 3,751,351 Ranked 28th state

\*Missouri

## STATE CAPITAL

Oklahoma City is the largest city in Oklahoma and one of the largest cities in the United States in terms of land area. Located on the North Canadian River, it became the state capital in 1910. Oil, transportation, and livestock are major contributors to Oklahoma City's economy. The city is a center for tourism and government in the state as well.

**Map Scale**

0            100 Miles

**N**

| LEGEND | |
| --- | --- |
| —— | Road |
| —— | River |
| ★ | State Capital |
| ● | City |
| ▨ | Oklahoma |
| ▬ | State Border |

**United States**

Hawai'i   Alaska

Oklahoma

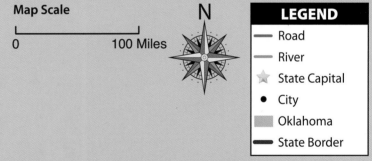

# The Land

The land in the Sooner State is vast and varied. It offers **fertile** farmland and forested mountain ranges. Elevations in the state range from 300 to 5,000 feet above sea level. The Ouachita Mountains, in southeastern Oklahoma, feature steep ridges and valleys. The Red River Plains, on the other hand, are low and flat. The High Plains are, of course, high. The land in this northwestern region is higher than the mountains to the east. Other parts of Oklahoma, such as the Ozark Plateau in the northeast, are made up of broad, flat-topped hills and narrow river valleys.

## WICHITA MOUNTAINS

Located in southwestern Oklahoma, the Wichita Mountains are thought to be hundreds of millions of years old. Huge boulders lie at the **summit** of Mount Scott, which rises 2,464 above sea level.

## RICH FARMLAND

Fertile farmland covers much of the eastern half of Oklahoma. Wheat is Oklahoma's largest crop and is grown on more than 3 million acres. Only three states produce more wheat than Oklahoma.

## RED RIVER

The Red River is 1,290 miles long. For about half that length it serves as the border between Oklahoma and Texas. Many dams have been built on the river to control flooding.

## SEQUOYAH NATIONAL WILDLIFE REFUGE

The Sequoyah National Wildlife Refuge is located in eastern Oklahoma, about 150 miles from Oklahoma City. Established in 1970, it is nestled in the rolling foothills of the Ozark Mountains. Its waters provide **habitat** for waterfowl and other migratory birds.

Summers in Oklahoma can be hot, humid, and windy.
July is the warmest month, with average high
temperatures around 82° Fahrenheit.

# Climate

**O**klahoma's climate is generally pleasant. The average annual temperature varies from about 57° Fahrenheit in the Panhandle to about 63° F in the southern part of the state.

The southeastern corner of Oklahoma receives average rainfall of about 56 inches a year, which is the most for any region in the state. In contrast, the Panhandle gets less than 20 inches of rainfall annually. The especially dry Panhandle often suffers **drought** and dust storms. Dozens of tornadoes touch down in Oklahoma each year, usually during the months of April and May.

## Average Annual Precipitation Across Oklahoma

There can be great variation in precipitation among different cities in Oklahoma. How does location affect the amount of rainfall a city receives?

**Inches of Rainfall**

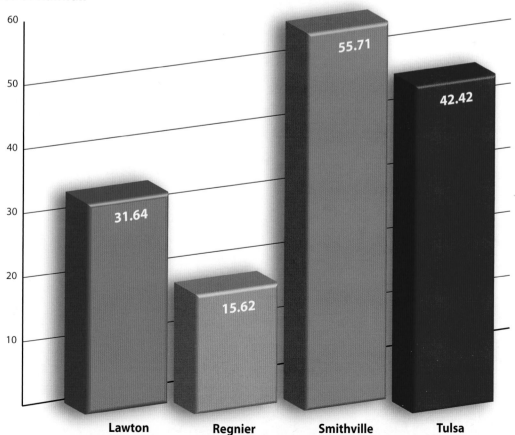

| City | Inches |
| --- | --- |
| Lawton | 31.64 |
| Regnier | 15.62 |
| Smithville | 55.71 |
| Tulsa | 42.42 |

# Natural Resources

Oklahoma has an abundance of natural resources. Forests in the Ouachita Mountains and along the Sandstone Hills provide a home for wildlife. These forests also provide trees for the lumber industry. On the prairies, crops such as oats, corn, and soybeans are grown in the northeast. Fields of wheat, barley, hay, and cotton are grown and harvested in the center of the state. Many regions are ideal for raising cattle. Of the nearly 34 million acres of farmland in the state, almost half is rangeland for livestock.

Pine timber dominates lumber production in Oklahoma, both in volume and economic importance. Pine forests in southeastern Oklahoma are expected to supply the industry with sustainable quantities of wood for many years to come.

Water is another important resource in Oklahoma. About 100 natural and 200 artificial lakes dot the state. Most of the lakes are fed by flowing rivers and streams. The two largest rivers are the Red and the Arkansas.

In terms of money brought into the state, mining is an extremely important industry in Oklahoma. The state's first major oil field was discovered near Tulsa in 1905. Since then oil or natural gas strikes have been made throughout Oklahoma. Large deposits of salt, coal, and gypsum are also mined. Other minerals found in the state include limestone, sand, gravel, granite, and clay.

Oklahoma's lakes provide opportunities for fishing, boating, and other watersports. Fish such as channel catfish, largemouth bass, walleye, and paddlefish inhabit the quiet waters of Fort Gibson Lake.

# I DIDN'T KNOW THAT!

**From 1988 to 1995** Oklahoma reduced the amount of toxic chemicals the state put into the environment by 55 percent.

**At one time** Oklahoma mined more than half of the world's supply of zinc. This resource has not been mined in the state since 1970.

**Trees cut down for lumber** in Oklahoma include pine, oak, walnut, hickory, and ash.

**There are about** 83,000 farms in Oklahoma. About 44 percent of Oklahoma's farmland is used to raise crops.

**The Pensacola Dam**, built in 1940, is still the world's longest multiple arch dam. At 6,565 feet in length, the dam is located on the south shore of Grand Lake O' the Cherokees between Langley and Disney.

# Plants

Forests and grasslands dominate much of Oklahoma's landscape. The state's largest forested areas are located in the east. More than 130 varieties of trees thrive in the state. Among these are longleaf pine, cottonwood, oak, hickory, juniper, and willow.

The plains regions, when not supporting farm crops, are covered in different kinds of grasses and wild plants. Sagebrush is common in this area, along with gramma, buffalo, Indian, and mesquite grasses. Wildflowers can be found in this area, too. They include black-eyed Susans, poppy mallows, wild indigos, prairie coneflowers, violets, wild roses, and prickly pear cacti.

## LONGLEAF PINES

The longleaf pine has the longest needles of any native North American pine. The needles grow in bundles of three and can reach a length of 18 inches. Longleaf pines take 100 to 150 years to grow to their full size and can live to be 300 years old.

## COTTONWOOD TREES

Cottonwood trees often grow beside streams or rivers. They can live to be 100 years old. Trees have either male or female flowers. The female trees bear fruit in a seed that is surrounded by a cotton-like material, which is how the tree got its name.

## SAGEBRUSH

Sagebrush are native to the semiarid plains of western North America, including in Oklahoma. The shrub has silver-gray leaves and usually grows to be 3 to 6 feet in height.

## BLACK-EYED SUSAN

The black-eyed Susan is one of the most common wildflowers in Oklahoma. Plants live for two years and bloom between June and October.

**The fruit and the pads** of the prickly pear cactus are edible. They are said to have health benefits.

**Another name for** the prairie coneflower is Mexican hat. The flower is native to the dry prairies of Oklahoma and other states.

**The Oklahoma wild rose** blooms in May on Oklahoma's tallgrass prairies. It is a climbing plant with stems that can be several feet long.

# Animals

In addition to the millions of head of cattle that roam the land, Oklahoma is home to many wild animals. Among poisonous snakes found slithering in Oklahoma are the rattlesnake, copperhead, and cottonmouth. Prairie dogs, raccoons, deer, antelope, gray squirrels, and fox squirrels also live in the state.

Many different kinds of birds nest in the state, including blue jays, mockingbirds, orioles, crows, roadrunners, and robins. Cardinals, meadowlarks, quail, wild turkeys, prairie chickens, and pheasant are also commonly found in the area. Oklahoma's many lakes and rivers are the habitat for a large variety of fish. Bass, catfish, carp, sunfish, drumfish, and paddlefish can all be found in Oklahoma's waters.

## BLACK-TAILED PRAIRIE DOG

Black-tailed prairie dogs are members of the squirrel family. They are social animals and live with other prairie dogs in burrows that have many openings. They are found in the western part of the state.

## CARP

Carp were first introduced to North America in 1877. Since then, they have become a common fish in many states, including Oklahoma. They typically weigh between 8 and 10 pounds.

## COPPERHEAD

The copperhead snake's bite is painful but usually not deadly. An adult copperhead can be 2 to 3 feet in length. It feeds on rodents, small birds, insects, lizards, and frogs.

## SCISSOR-TAILED FLYCATCHER

The scissor-tailed flycatcher is the state bird. Oklahoma is at the center of this bird's breeding area. The scissor-tailed flycatcher uses many human-made products in its nest, including string, cloth, paper, and carpet fuzz.

**The fox squirrel** is found across most of Oklahoma. It is burnt orange in color with a gray back. Fox squirrels can weigh up to 3 pounds. It is one of the 2 species of squirrel that is legal to hunt in Oklahoma.

**Roadrunners are** a common sight on the plains of Oklahoma. Insects and reptiles make up most of their diet.

**The Selman Bat Cave** in northwest Oklahoma is the summer home of more than 1 million Mexican free-tailed bats. The bats eat 10 tons of insects every night.

**The white, or sand,** bass is the state fish, and the mountain boomer lizard is the state reptile.

**The paddlefish** has an unusual snout, which is long and flat and looks like a paddle. The paddlefish is found in the Grand, Neosho, and Arkansas river systems in Oklahoma.

# Tourism

**V**acationers come to the Sooner State to enjoy its natural beauty, outdoor activities, and much more. In the summer tourists can visit Oklahoma's many lakes to enjoy fishing, boating, waterskiing, sailing, or windsurfing. Resorts can also be found along some of the larger lakes, where patrons can golf, play tennis, dine in great restaurants, and stay in cottages or hotels.

Nature lovers and history buffs appreciate Oklahoma's many attractions and recreational areas. Visitors can choose to explore any of the state's two national parks, 32 state parks, 28 state recreation areas, or 48 wildlife management areas. There are many museums and cultural sites in the state, too. At the Anadarko Basin Museum of Natural History in Elk City, visitors can view rocks, minerals, and fossils.

## NATIONAL COWBOY & WESTERN HERITAGE MUSEUM

The National Cowboy & Western Heritage Museum collects and exhibits art and artifacts of the American West. Since the museum was founded in 1955, more than 10 million people from around the world have visited it.

## FIVE CIVILIZED TRIBES MUSEUM

The Five Civilized Tribes Museum in Muskogee is dedicated to preserving the history and culture of tribes forced to move from farther east in the early 1800s. They are the Cherokee, Chickasaw, Choctaw, Muscogee (Creek), and Seminole people.

## TULSA ZOO AND LIVING MUSEUM

The Tulsa Zoo and Living Museum features more than 2,800 animals on 84 acres of land. In the Africa exhibit, visitors can see golden crowned cranes in addition to cheetahs, lions, giraffes, and zebras.

## WICHITA MOUNTAINS NATIONAL WILDLIFE REFUGE

The Wichita Mountains are home to one of the United States' earliest wildlife refuges. Established in 1901, Wichita Mountains National Wildlife Refuge shelters Texas longhorn cattle, buffalo, deer, elk, coyotes, prairie dogs, and turkeys.

## I DIDN'T KNOW THAT!

**Visitors in Oklahoma City** can tour the National Softball Hall of Fame and the International Photography Hall of Fame and Museum.

**The Gilcrease Museum** in Tulsa houses a large collection of art and artifacts of the American West.

**Events such as rodeos** and horse shows draw people to Oklahoma.

**Oklahoma City's Bricktown** is an entertainment district that features restaurants, shops, sporting facilities, and a canal for people to stroll along.

**The Trail of Tears** National Historic Trail ended in Oklahoma. Visitors can find out more about the Cherokees who traveled the trail in the 1830s.

# Industry

**M**ining accounts for a much larger share of the economy in Oklahoma than in most other states. Of all 50 states, Oklahoma is the third-largest producer of marketable natural gas and the sixth-largest producer of oil. Manufacturing is also extremely important, contributing almost as much to the economy as mining does.

## Industries in Oklahoma
### Value of Goods and Services in Millions of Dollars

The mining of oil and natural gas is now very important to the state's economy. As supplies of oil and gas go down over time, what other types of energy-related industries might develop in Oklahoma to make up for reduced oil and gas income?

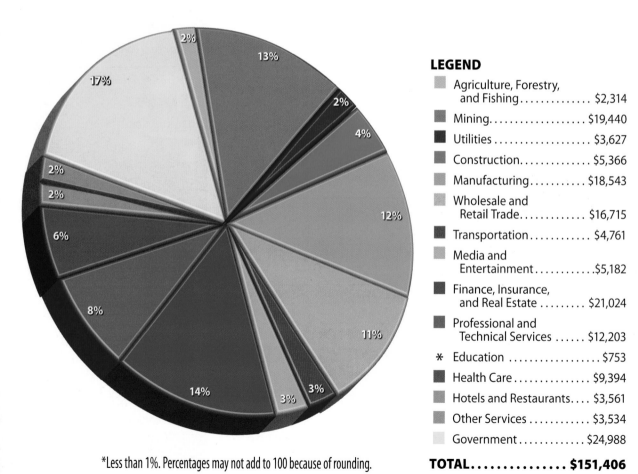

**LEGEND**

| | | |
|---|---|---|
| | Agriculture, Forestry, and Fishing | $2,314 |
| | Mining | $19,440 |
| | Utilities | $3,627 |
| | Construction | $5,366 |
| | Manufacturing | $18,543 |
| | Wholesale and Retail Trade | $16,715 |
| | Transportation | $4,761 |
| | Media and Entertainment | $5,182 |
| | Finance, Insurance, and Real Estate | $21,024 |
| | Professional and Technical Services | $12,203 |
| * | Education | $753 |
| | Health Care | $9,394 |
| | Hotels and Restaurants | $3,561 |
| | Other Services | $3,534 |
| | Government | $24,988 |
| | **TOTAL** | **$151,406** |

*Less than 1%. Percentages may not add to 100 because of rounding.

Factories in the state manufacture machinery, transportation equipment, food products, and rubber and plastic products. The state also produces electrical equipment, mobile homes, and glass and clay products. Tulsa and Oklahoma counties are the most important manufacturing areas.

Oklahoma's diversified industrial base helps keep the economy stable, even in times of failed crops and low oil or cattle prices. Many oil-producing areas of the state often have another strong industry to balance the economy of the region. For example, while Tulsa has more than 1,000 oil-based companies, it also has a strong **aerospace industry**.

*Oil was first discovered in Oklahoma before it became a state. Oklahoma's major oil fields have produced more than 100 million barrels of oil.*

**Oklahoma** is known as a livestock state. More than 5 million head of cattle are raised in the state each year.

**Oil, natural gas, and coal** account for 95 percent of the state's mining **revenue**.

**Oklahoma manufactures** machinery needed by the oil and gas industries. This includes equipment used in oil extraction, such as pumps, pipes, and valves.

**Another important** industry in Oklahoma is the production of electrical equipment, especially for use in communications.

# Goods and Services

**M**any of the finished products manufactured in Oklahoma are transported to other parts of the country. Besides the three interstate highways that cross the state, Oklahoma has many miles of railroad tracks to transport goods into and out of the area.

Food products are important to Oklahoma's economy. Flour mills operate in various locations in the state. Canneries package or freeze fruits and vegetables in many of the state's eastern cities. Creameries, ice cream plants, and bakeries supply treats and sweets to Oklahomans statewide. Meat packaging plants are found in many Oklahoma cities, including Tulsa, Durant, Oklahoma City, and Ada.

Interstate 35 is a key transportation route running north-south across the state, and Interstate 40 runs east-west. Interstate 44 is a toll road running from northeastern to southwestern Oklahoma. Oklahoma is second only to Florida in the number of miles of toll roads in the state.

*The aerospace industry is an important component of Oklahoma's economy. It is responsible for more than 143,000 jobs in the state and has a $5 billion dollar annual payroll.*

Oklahoma has a number of successful high-technology industries as well. The state is a national leader in the aerospace industry. More than 140,000 workers are employed by the more than 65 aerospace companies in the state. These companies include giants such as Boeing, Lockheed Martin, and Learjet. Tinker Air Force Base, located near Oklahoma City, employs thousands of workers and brings more than $2 billion into the state each year. Biotechnology companies in the state produce medical devices, medicines, and other products.

Services provide more jobs in Oklahoma than any other part of the economy. About two-thirds of Oklahoma's workers are employed in this sector, which includes a wide range of jobs, such as teachers, health-care workers, computer programmers, store clerks, hotel staffs, and government workers.

# American Indians

**E**arly American Indians known as Mound Builders lived close to the Arkansas-Oklahoma border from around AD 800 to 1400. Traces of the culture of the Mound Builders can still be found from central Georgia to southern Mississippi. The Mound Builders built large hills out of earth and used them as platforms for homes and as sites for their temples. Digging out the mounds has resulted in many finds. **Archaeologists** have uncovered pottery, textiles, and metalwork that display a high level of skill.

When Europeans arrived in the mid-1500s, a number of American Indian groups lived in what is now Oklahoma. Together these groups were known as the Plains Indians. In the east the Kiowa, the Plains Apache, and the Comanche hunted bison, or buffalo, on the prairie. The Caddo, the Wichita, the Pawnee, the Osage, and the Quapaw also lived in the Oklahoma region.

Peskelechaco was a chief of the Pawnee tribe in the early 1800s. Like other Plains Indians, the Pawnee lived in earth-covered lodges most of the year but used tepees while on buffalo hunts. Pawnee women raised corn, squash, and beans and were experts at making pottery.

As the number of people of European descent living in the eastern United States steadily increased, these settlers pressured the U.S. government to push American Indian groups in the East off the land. In 1828 the U.S. Congress reserved the Oklahoma area for Indians and required all settlers to leave. The land would later be named Indian Territory. Between 1830 and 1848 five tribes from the Southeast were **relocated** to this area. These were the Seminole, the Cherokee, the Chickasaw, the Choctaw, and the Creek. They set up their own system of government, which was the first organized system of government in Oklahoma. They were referred to as the Five Civilized Tribes.

Later, more Indians moved to the region, and about 60 groups soon shared the land. By 1907, though, American Indians had lost most of their land in Oklahoma. Today 35 tribal governments are based in the state.

Men of the Choctaw tribe played a traditional ball game with rackets and goalposts. Hundreds of players would take part in one game, as other members of the tribe made bets on the outcome.

*In 1541, the Spanish explorer Hernando de Soto and his followers reached the Mississippi River. They went on to explore a region that now forms part of Arkansas, Oklahoma, and northern Texas.*

# Explorers

The written history of Oklahoma dates back to 1541. Spanish explorers called conquistadores came to North America during the mid-1500s hoping to find gold and silver. The explorer Francisco Vázquez de Coronado was the first European to enter what is now Oklahoma. Other Spanish explorers followed, all in search of the legendary golden Seven Cities of Cíbola. Although no golden cities were found, Coronado claimed the western part of the Mississippi River Valley for Spain. Another Spanish explorer, Hernando de Soto, laid claim to the lower Mississippi Valley for Spain. But Spain eventually lost control of the region to France.

In 1682, René-Robert Cavelier, sieur de La Salle, traveled south from the Great Lakes to the mouth of the Mississippi at the Gulf of Mexico. On behalf of the king of France, he claimed all the lands drained by the Mississippi River and its **tributaries**. This included the land that is now Oklahoma. French fur traders quickly made their way to the Oklahoma area, settling along the Red and Arkansas rivers.

# Timeline of Settlement

## Early Exploration

**1541** Francisco Vázquez de Coronado explores the Oklahoma region for Spain.

**1682** René-Robert Cavelier, sieur de La Salle, claims land, including what is now Oklahoma, for France.

## Indian Territory

**1803** The United States purchases the Louisiana Territory, including Oklahoma, from France.

**1830** Indian Territory is established in present-day Oklahoma.

**1830–1848** The Five Civilized Tribes are forced to move to Indian Territory.

## Arrival of Settlers

**1866** Cowboys begin driving cattle across Oklahoma.

**1870** The Missouri, Kansas, and Texas Railroad begins laying tracks into Indian Territory.

**1875** Cattle ranches are established in western Indian Territory.

## Road to Statehood

**1889** The Great Land Rush opens Oklahoma to large-scale settlement by people of European descent.

**1890** The U.S. government creates the Oklahoma Territory.

**1906** The Oklahoma and Indian territories are combined.

**1907** Oklahoma becomes the 46th state.

# Early Settlers

O klahoma became part of the United States through the Louisiana Purchase in 1803. Although white settlement was forbidden in the area between 1828 and 1889, inroads were made in the form of forts, schools for American Indians, and cattle trails. Some adventurers and farmers also entered the territory. Part of Indian Territory was opened up for white settlement in 1889.

## Map of Settlements and Resources in Early Oklahoma

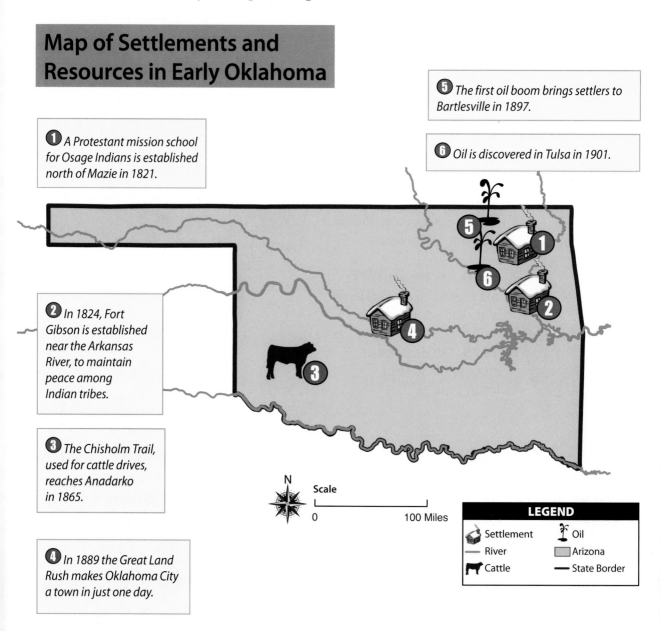

❺ The first oil boom brings settlers to Bartlesville in 1897.

❻ Oil is discovered in Tulsa in 1901.

❶ A Protestant mission school for Osage Indians is established north of Mazie in 1821.

❷ In 1824, Fort Gibson is established near the Arkansas River, to maintain peace among Indian tribes.

❸ The Chisholm Trail, used for cattle drives, reaches Anadarko in 1865.

❹ In 1889 the Great Land Rush makes Oklahoma City a town in just one day.

N
Scale
0       100 Miles

**LEGEND**

| | |
|---|---|
| Settlement | Oil |
| River | Arizona |
| Cattle | State Border |

Two million acres of the territory were made available to homesteaders on April 22, 1889. At noon that day, a single shot marked the beginning of the land run. Fifty thousand people rushed to stake their land claims. In just one day Oklahoma City was created. About 10,000 people pitched their tents and set up shelters in this area. Another 15,000 stopped at what is now Guthrie. This new town became the state's first capital.

*Many of the early settlers' dwellings in Oklahoma were made out of sod. Sod houses were constructed from stacked layers of squarely cut earth, shaped much like bricks. Settlers had to build sod houses because it was difficult to find trees on the plains.*

**After the American Civil War**, great cattle drives followed the Chisholm Trail, which ran from San Antonio, Texas, through Oklahoma to Abilene, Kansas. From there beef was shipped to cities in the East. During this time Oklahoma was part of the Wild West.

**After the Great Land Rush** of 1889, there were more land runs. Each one took more of Indian Territory from the American Indians.

**The largest land rush** was in 1893, when 6 million acres were opened for settlement.

# Notable People

**M**any notable Oklahomans have contributed to the development of their state and their country. Some people have become writers, songwriters, or film directors, describing the American experience. Others became humorists or psychologists, helping people tackle life's problems. Still others have become scientists and adventurers such as astronauts.

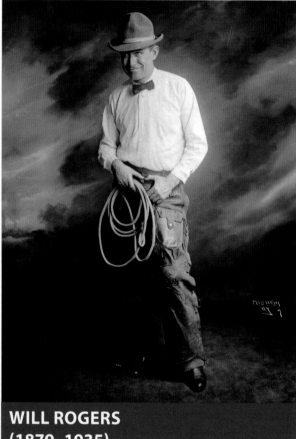

## WILL ROGERS (1879–1935)

Will Rogers was a popular entertainer of the early 20th century. He was born in Oologah to parents who were part Cherokee. As a young man, he began performing roping skills in Wild West shows. Audiences loved his homespun humor, and Rogers expanded his career into acting and writing. He is known for his amusing observations about people, the country, and government.

## WOODY GUTHRIE (1912–1967)

Born in Okemah, Woody Guthrie became a well-known singer and writer of folk songs. In the 1930s, during the Great Depression, Guthrie developed great compassion for people in need. This was evident in many of his songs. Guthrie strongly influenced folk singers of the 1960s, including his son Arlo. Woody Guthrie's most popular song is "This Land Is Your Land."

## RALPH ELLISON
## (1914–1994)

Born in Oklahoma City, Ralph Ellison published his first novel, *Invisible Man*, in 1953. The novel is about a young African American man who finds he is ignored because of his race. It is noteworthy for its exposure of racism in 20th-century America. *Invisible Man* won the National Book Award for fiction.

## SHANNON LUCID
## (1943–)

Shannon Lucid grew up in Bethany and became a biochemist and an astronaut. She flew on five space shuttle missions. In 1996, she spent 188 days on the Russian space station *Mir*. At that time this set a record for the longest time spent in space by any astronaut. Lucid continues to work for the National Aeronautics and Space Administration.

## DR. PHIL McGRAW
## (1950–)

Born in Vinita, Phil McGraw became a psychologist and started a company to help lawyers by using psychology. Through his company, he met Oprah Winfrey, and he became a frequent guest on her TV show. In 2002, McGraw started his own television show, *Dr. Phil*. Viewers and participants like his no-nonsense approach to solving life's problems.

**Wilma Mankiller (1945–2010)** was principal chief of the Cherokee Nation from 1985 to 1995. She worked to improve the lives of her people by seeking better health care, improving adult literacy, and attracting industry to the Cherokee Nation. She was the first woman to serve as chief of the Cherokee Nation.

**Ron Howard (1954– )** was born in Duncan and has been involved in TV and films most of his life. He acted in *The Andy Griffith Show* as a child and in *Happy Days* as a young man. As a director, Howard won an Academy Award for Best Director in 2001 for his film *A Beautiful Mind*.

# Population

According to the 2010 U.S. Census, more than 3.7 million people lived in Oklahoma as of April 1 of that year. Between 2000 and 2010, Oklahoma's population increased by about 300,000 people, or 8.7 percent. This was a slightly lower rate of growth than the national average, which was 9.7 percent. Nearly 65 percent of Oklahomans live in urban areas, in cities or towns. There are 33 cities with populations of more than 15,000 people.

## Oklahoma Population 1950–2010

Oklahoma gained about 225,000 residents between 1950 and 1970. From 1990 to 2010, the population grew by more than 600,000 people. What factors might account for the difference in population growth in these two 20-year periods?

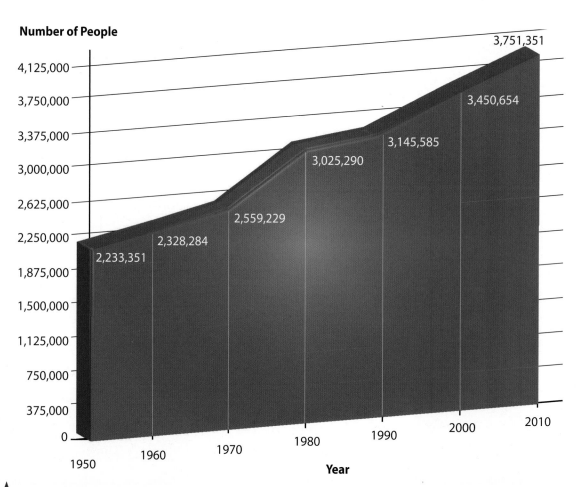

**Number of People**

| Year | Population |
|------|-----------|
| 1950 | 2,233,351 |
| 1960 | 2,328,284 |
| 1970 | 2,559,229 |
| 1980 | 3,025,290 |
| 1990 | 3,145,585 |
| 2000 | 3,450,654 |
| 2010 | 3,751,351 |

**Year**

Oklahoma's Hispanic population almost doubled between 2000 and 2010. Groups such as the Greater Oklahoma City Hispanic Chamber of Commerce help people develop and promote new businesses.

The residents of the Sooner State come from many different racial and **ethnic** backgrounds. About 78 percent of Oklahomans are of European heritage. Of all 50 states, Oklahoma ranks third in the number of American Indians in its population.

Until the 1960s almost all Hispanics in Oklahoma were of Mexican descent. Beginning in the 1960s the non-Mexican Hispanic population of Oklahoma grew. Puerto Ricans now make up the second-largest Hispanic group in Oklahoma. A smaller percentage of Hispanics are of Cuban descent.

Almost one-fourth of all Oklahomans are under the age of 18.

The Oklahoma State Capitol was built between 1914 and 1917 at a cost $1.5 million. The Capitol building is mainly composed of white limestone with a base of Oklahoma pink granite. In front of the building is a sculpture of a cowboy on a bucking bronco, representing the state's cowboy heritage.

# Politics and Government

Oklahoma's government consists of three branches. The governor heads the executive branch, which makes sure that laws are carried out. The governor appoints a number of high-level state officials, such as the secretary of state, the secretary of finance, and other state commissioners.

The legislative branch, or state legislature, consists of two chambers, or parts. They are the Senate and the House of Representatives. The 48 senators and the 101 members of the House of Representatives make the laws of the state, but residents may also propose new laws.

The judicial branch is made up of the state's courts. The highest-level court is the Supreme Court. The judicial branch also includes the court of criminal appeals and the court of appeals. It is the duty of each judge within these courts to interpret the laws of the state.

In the U.S. Congress, Oklahoma, like all other states, has two senators in the U.S. Senate. Oklahoma has five members in the U.S. House of Representatives, where the number of seats each state has depends on its population.

In 2011, Mary Fallin became Oklahoma's first female governor and the 27th governor of the state. Previously, she served in the U.S. Congress from 2006 to 2011.

# Cultural Groups

Indian Territory was the final stop for many American Indian tribes forced from the southeastern states. Today Oklahoma's American Indians work to preserve their cultures and customs. Traditional dance exhibitions and large gatherings called **powwows** are held every summer and fall across the state.

The cowboy culture that emerged in the 1800s is still alive in Oklahoma. Rodeos once served as a way for cowboys to keep up their ranching skills. Now, few cowboys use these skills for actual ranching. Instead they train and compete for cash prizes. Today's rodeos owe some of their traditions to the original Wild West shows, which also included riding and roping demonstrations.

Powwows are social gatherings of American Indians who follow traditional dances started hundreds of years ago by their ancestors. Many Indians also take advantage of the opportunity to see old friends and teach traditional ways to a younger generation.

Pawnee Bill's Wild West Show is an adaptation of the original Wild West shows from the early 1900s. The show in Pawnee features cowboys and Indians, traditional costumes, and an array of activities. A favorite event is cowboys performing tricks with their lassos.

With modern advances, ranching life has changed. Today many ranchers use less traditional methods in raising cattle. Trucks are more common than horses, and even helicopters may be used to herd cattle.

African Americans have played an important role in Oklahoma's cultural development, especially in terms of music. Blues, gospel, and jazz can be heard across the state. In the 1920s jazz boomed in the Second Street area, known as Deep Deuce, in Oklahoma City. Today people of many different backgrounds come together to celebrate this rich African American musical heritage by attending jazz, gospel, and blues music festivals.

## I DIDN'T KNOW THAT!

**The drum** is a very important part of traditional American Indian dances. People sit around one large drum, strike it, and chant while dances are performed. Many Indians consider the drum to be "the heartbeat of the people."

**The Red Earth Festival,** which takes place every June in Oklahoma City, is the state's largest annual American Indian gathering. More than 100 tribes participate in the event.

**Jazz lovers can** listen to cool tunes every August at Jazz on Greenwood in Tulsa.

**The Oklahoma Czech** Festival in Yukon takes place on the first Saturday in October. Czech culture is celebrated with traditional foods and dancers.

**One of the longest-running** African American rodeos is held each year in Okmulgee.

**Blues fans head** to the historic town of Rentiesville to catch the Dusk 'Til Dawn Blues Festival every September.

**While in Tulsa**, residents and tourists can visit the Oklahoma Jazz Hall of Fame.

# Arts and Entertainment

T he arts are an important part of Oklahoma's culture. In fact, according to state law, the arts must be taught in all schools. The Oklahoma Arts Council works to keep the arts **accessible** to all state residents. The group sponsors community arts projects and performances.

American Indian arts and crafts can be found across the state. Traditional crafts such as beadwork, featherwork, and jewelry-making are still practiced. Native crafts and artwork can be seen at the Southern Plains Indian Museum in Anadarko. Art lovers can also find modern American Indian paintings and sculptures at Muskogee's Five Civilized Tribes Museum.

The Cherokee National Museum in Tahlequah was designed by Cherokee architect Charles Chief Boyd. The design symbolizes a traditional Cherokee dwelling, built low to the ground and illuminated at both ends by natural lighting. The museum houses a permanent Trail of Tears exhibit, two major art shows each year, and a center for tracing Cherokee descent.

Many well-known singers and musicians hail from Oklahoma. A number of the state's country and western stars have become national celebrities. Country music performers from Oklahoma include Carrie Underwood from Muskogee, Garth Brooks from Tulsa, Vince Gill from Norman, and Reba McEntire from McAlester.

Carrie Underwood dreamed of being a singer. She launched her career by appearing on the television show *American Idol*. Garth Brooks began his music career while attending Oklahoma State University in Stillwater. He started performing at a local club called Tumbleweeds. Vince Gill's music career began at an even earlier age. He was a member of a high school band. Reba McEntire began singing as a child, in a family band called the Singing McEntires. She sang with her brothers and sisters in clubs and community centers around McAlester. Oklahoma is also the birthplace of some first-rate opera singers, including Leona Mitchell, Chris Merritt, and David Pittman-Jennings.

*Carrie Underwood was born in Muskogee and raised on a farm. She released her first album in 2005. Four years later, she won the Grammy for Best Female Country Vocal Performance for her song "Last Name."*

# Sports

In 2008, a National Basketball Association, or NBA, team relocated to Oklahoma City. The Oklahoma City Thunder moved from Seattle, where the team had been called the Seattle SuperSonics. Led by forward Kevin Durant, the Thunder made it to the playoffs in its second season of operation in Oklahoma.

Oklahoma has produced some incredible athletes. Many of baseball's greats have come from the Sooner State. They include Hall of Famers Mickey Mantle, Johnny Bench, Dizzy Dean, Warren Spahn, and Willie Stargell.

Oklahomans strongly support their college sports teams. This includes cheering for the football teams at two of the state's largest universities, the University of Oklahoma and Oklahoma State University. Together these schools can boast the attendance of Football Hall of Famers Lee Roy Selmon, Tommy McDonald, Thurman Thomas, and Barry Sanders.

*Kevin Durant is an All-Star forward for the NBA's Oklahoma City Thunder. In 2009–2010 he was named to the First Team All-NBA. He is the youngest player in NBA history to win the scoring title, with 30.1 points per game that year.*

Many other top athletes have come from Oklahoma. They include golfer Nancy Lopez Wright, baseball star Joe Carter, football star Troy Aikman, gymnast Shannon Miller, rodeo star Jim Shoulders, and wrestler John Smith.

The University of Oklahoma Sooners football team has a long tradition of success and has won a number of national championships. In 2011 they won the Tostitos Fiesta Bowl, playing against the University of Connecticut. Quarterback Landry Jones threw for 429 yards and 3 touchdowns.

# I DIDN'T KNOW THAT!

**Shannon Miller** is the most decorated American gymnast in history. She is a seven-time Olympic medalist and won two World All-Around gold medals.

**One of Oklahoma's** most famous athletes was Jim Thorpe. This Oklahoman of American Indian heritage won eight gold medals at the Olympic Games in 1912.

**Former Olympian Nadia Comaneci** and her husband, Bart Conner, run a gymnastics school in Oklahoma, Conner's home state.

**Mickey Mantle** was **inducted** into the Baseball Hall of Fame in 1974.

**Jim Shoulders** won a record 16 world rodeo championship events.

**With seating** for more than 82,000 fans, the University of Oklahoma's Memorial Stadium is home to the Sooners football team.

# National Averages Comparison

T he United States is a federal republic, consisting of fifty states and the District of Columbia. Alaska and Hawai'i are the only non-contiguous, or non-touching, states in the nation. Today, the United States of America is the third-largest country in the world in population. The United States Census Bureau takes a census, or count of all the people, every ten years. It also regularly collects other kinds of data about the population and the economy. How does Oklahoma compare to the national average?

## Comparison Chart

| Statistic | USA | Oklahoma |
|---|---|---|
| Admission to Union | NA | November 16, 1907 |
| Land Area (in square miles) | 3,537,438.44 | 68,667.06 |
| Population Total | 308,745,538 | 3,751,351 |
| Population Density (people per square mile) | 87.28 | 54.63 |
| Population Percentage Change (April 1, 2000, to April 1, 2010) | 9.7% | 8.7% |
| White Persons (percent) | 72.4% | 72.2% |
| Black Persons (percent) | 12.6% | 7.4% |
| American Indian and Alaska Native Persons (percent) | 0.9% | 8.6% |
| Asian Persons (percent) | 4.8% | 1.7% |
| Native Hawaiian and Other Pacific Islander Persons (percent) | 0.2% | 0.1% |
| Some Other Race (percent) | 6.2% | 4.1% |
| Persons Reporting Two or More Races (percent) | 2.9% | 5.9% |
| Persons of Hispanic or Latino Origin (percent) | 16.3% | 8.9% |
| Not of Hispanic or Latino Origin (percent) | 83.7% | 91.1% |
| Median Household Income | $52,029 | $42,836 |
| Percentage of People Age 25 or Over Who Have Graduated from High School | 80.4% | 80.6% |

*All figures are based on the 2010 United States Census, with the exception of the last two items.

# How to Improve My Community

**S**trong communities make strong states. Think about what features are important in your community. What do you value? Education? Health? Forests? Safety? Beautiful spaces? Government works to help citizens create ideal living conditions that are fair to all by providing services in communities. Consider what changes you could make in your community. How would they improve your state as a whole? Using this concept web as a guide, write a report that outlines the features you think are most important in your community and what improvements could be made. A strong state needs strong communities.

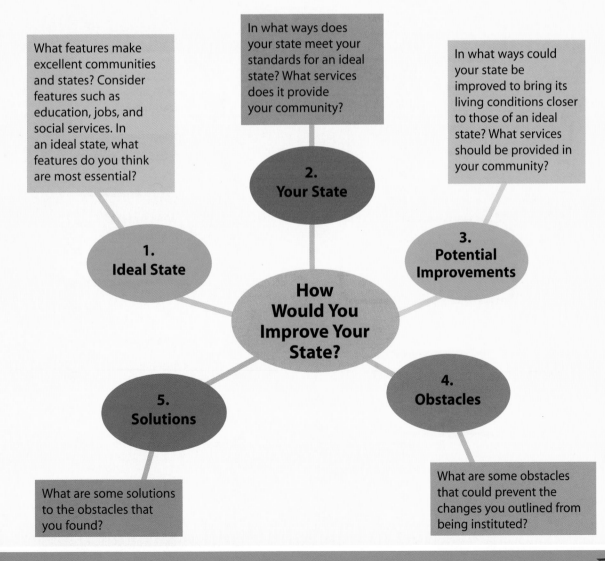

What features make excellent communities and states? Consider features such as education, jobs, and social services. In an ideal state, what features do you think are most essential?

In what ways does your state meet your standards for an ideal state? What services does it provide your community?

In what ways could your state be improved to bring its living conditions closer to those of an ideal state? What services should be provided in your community?

**2.
Your State**

**1.
Ideal State**

**3.
Potential
Improvements**

**How
Would You
Improve Your
State?**

**5.
Solutions**

**4.
Obstacles**

What are some solutions to the obstacles that you found?

What are some obstacles that could prevent the changes you outlined from being instituted?

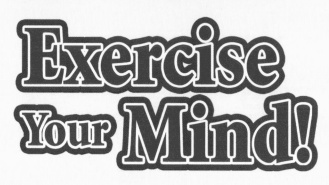
# Exercise Your Mind!

Think about these questions and then use your research skills to find the answers and learn more fascinating facts about Oklahoma. A teacher, librarian, or parent may be able to help you locate the best sources to use in your research.

**1** One African American cowboy became popular during the days of the Wild West. Who was he?

**2** Where was the first parking meter installed?

**3** Where can visitors to Oklahoma learn about the state's early oil boom?

**4** How is Oklahoma divided into six different "countries"?

**5** Name Oklahoma's four mountain ranges.

**6** Which American Indian groups were called the Five Civilized Tribes?

**7** What historic highway runs through Oklahoma?

**8** Name writer Ralph Ellison's most famous work.

# Words to Know

**accessible:** easy to approach, available

**aerospace industry:** the research, design, and production of airplanes, missiles, and spacecraft

**archaeologists:** scientists who study the cultures of early peoples through artifacts and remains

**capitol:** the building where a legislature meets

**diverse:** varied, having differences

**drought:** an extended period with very little or no rain

**ethnic:** relating to a group of people who share a common culture

**fertile:** ground rich in materials that help plants to growth well

**habitat:** the place where a plant or animal normally lives

**heritage:** ancestry, or a person's cultural background

**inducted:** admitted as a member

**mural:** a large painting that is painted directly on a wall or ceiling

**powwows:** American Indian ceremonies or social gatherings

**relocated:** moved to a new location

**revenue:** income

**summit:** the highest point, as of a mountain

**tributaries:** streams feeding larger bodies of water

# Index

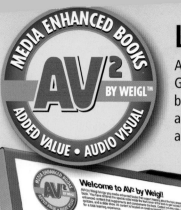

# Log on to www.av2books.com

AV² by Weigl brings you media enhanced books that support active learning. Go to www.av2books.com, and enter the special code found on page 2 of this book. You will gain access to enriched and enhanced content that supplements and complements this book. Content includes video, audio, web links, quizzes, a slide show, and activities.

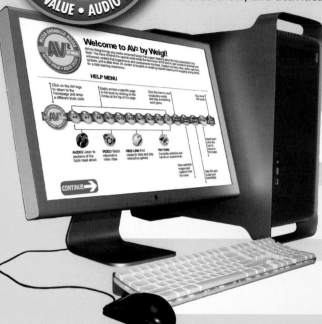

**Audio**
Listen to sections of the book read aloud.

**Video**
Watch informative video clips.

**Embedded Weblinks**
Gain additional information for research.

**Try This!**
Complete activities and hands-on experiments.

# WHAT'S ONLINE?

|  Try This! |  Embedded Weblinks |  Video | EXTRA FEATURES |
|---|---|---|---|
| Test your knowledge of the state in a mapping activity. | Discover more attractions in Oklahoma. | Watch a video introduction to Oklahoma. |  **Audio** Listen to sections of the book read aloud. |
| Find out more about precipitation in your city. | Learn more about the history of the state. | Watch a video about the features of the state. | |
| Plan what attractions you would like to visit in the state. | Learn the full lyrics of the state song. | |  **Key Words** Study vocabulary, and complete a matching word activity. |
| Learn more about the early natural resources of the state. | | | |
| Write a biography about a notable resident of Oklahoma. | | |  **Slide Show** View images and captions, and prepare a presentation. |
| Complete an educational census activity. | | | |
| | | |  **Quizzes** Test your knowledge. |

**AV² was built to bridge the gap between print and digital. We encourage you to tell us what you like and what you want to see in the future.**
**Sign up to be an AV² Ambassador at www.av2books.com/ambassador.**

Due to the dynamic nature of the Internet, some of the URLs and activities provided as part of AV² by Weigl may have changed or ceased to exist. AV² by Weigl accepts no responsibility for any such changes. All media enhanced books are regularly monitored to update addresses and sites in a timely manner. Contact AV² by Weigl at 1-866-649-3445 or av2books@weigl.com with any questions, comments, or feedback.